Penguin Readers

TAYLOR SWIFT

HANNAH DOLAN

T0116715

LEVEL

1

SERIES EDITOR: SORREL PITTS

PENGUIN BOOKS

UK | USA | Canada | Ireland | Australia
India | New Zealand | South Africa

Penguin Books is part of the Penguin Random House group of companies
whose addresses can be found at global.penguinrandomhouse.com.
www.penguin.co.uk www.puffin.co.uk www.ladybird.co.uk

Penguin
Random House
UK

First published 2020
003

Text written by Hannah Dolan
Text copyright © Penguin Books Ltd, 2020

Photo credits:

cover and page 9 (Taylor in Tokyo) © Jun Sato/TAS18/Getty Images; page 4 (Taylor Swift) © C Flanigan/Getty Images; (Andrea Swift) ©
Rick Diamond/ACMA2013/Getty Images for ACM; (Scott Swift) © Rick Diamond/ACMA2013/Getty Images for ACM;
(Austin Swift) © Rick Diamond/Getty Images; (Selena Gomez) © C Flanigan/Getty Images; (cats) © Raymond Hall/GC Images/Getty
Images; Page 5 (boyfriend) © Vital9s/Shutterstock; (CD) © panchof/Getty Images; (fans) © Jun Sato/TAS18/Getty Images; (stadium) ©
Christian Bertrand/Shutterstock; (stage) © Rick Diamond/WireImage/Getty Images; page 7 (fans at the Tokyo Dome) © Jun Sato/
TAS18/Getty Images; page 8 (Taylor on her *Reputation* tour) © Jun Sato/TAS18/Getty Images; page 10/11 (Christmas tree farm) © H.
Mark Weidman Photography / Alamy Stock Photo; page 11 (Taylor and Austin Swift) © Rick Diamond/Getty Images; page 12 (horses and
dog) © KatherinAmber/Shutterstock; page 13 (Wyomissing) © cwieders/Shutterstock; page 14 (Charlie and the Chocolate Factory cover) ©
Penguin Random House; page 15 (theatre) © Ververidis Vasilis/Shutterstock; page 16/17 (Taylor singing national anthem in 2002) © Jesse
D. Garrabrant/NBAE via Getty Images; page 18 (Faith Hill) © Frank Micelotta Archive/ImageDirect/Getty Images; page 19 (Nashville) ©
Mira / Alamy Stock Photo; page 20 (Dolly Parton) © Brett Carlsen/Getty Images; page 21 (LeAnn Rimes) © Michael Caulfield Archive/
WireImage/Getty Images; (Shania Twain) © Mick Hutson/Redferns/Getty Images; page 22 (Music Square) © Images-USA / Alamy Stock
Photo; page 23 (Musicians in Nashville) © Jon Hicks/Getty Images; page 24 (Taylor with a guitar) © Startraks/Shutterstock; page 25
(Taylor) © Ethan Miller/Getty Images; page 26 (Dan Dymtrow) © J.Sciulli/WireImage for Jive Records/Getty images; page 27 (RCA's
office in Nashville) © Andrew Woodley/Universal Images Group via Getty Images; page 28/29 (Hendersonville) © Michael S. Williamson/
The Washington Post via Getty Images; page 29 (Liz Rose) © Christian Petersen/Getty Images; page 30 (Taylor at 15) © Michael
Loccisano/FilmMagic/Getty Images; page 31 (Bluebird Café) © Bruce Yuanyue Bi/Getty Images; (Scott Borchetta) © Michael Tran/Getty
Images; page 32 (Taylor and Scott) © Larry Busacca/TAS/Getty Images for TAS; page 33 (Tim McGraw) © Tim Mosenfelder/Corbis via
Getty Images; page 34 (Young Taylor) © Rick Diamond/WireImage/Getty Images; page 35 (Taylor's Instagram page) © Mykhailo Polenok
/ Alamy Stock Photo; page 36/37 (Taylor on television) © Startraks/Shutterstock; page 38 (Taylor with Faith Hill and Tim McGraw) ©
Kevin Winter/ACMA/Getty Images for ACMA; page 39 (on Faith and Tim's tour) © ZUMA Press, Inc. / Alamy Stock Photo; page 40/41
(Taylor with her award) © Peter Kramer/Getty Images; page 41 (at the Grammys in 2008) © Startraks/Shutterstock; page 42 (Taylor on
her *Fearless* tour) © Jason Kempin/Getty Images; page 43 (Taylor singing in a stadium) © Everett Collection/Shutterstock; page 44 (Taylor's
Swifties) © Bryan Bedder/Getty Images; page 45 (T-party) © Larry Busacca/TAS/Getty Images for TAS; page 46 (Kanye West) ©
Christopher Polk/Getty Images; page 47 (Beyoncé and Taylor) © Jeff Kravitz/FilmMagic/Getty Images; page 48 (Selena and Taylor) ©
Kevin Mazur/Getty Images for iHeartRadio/Turner; (Taylor's friends) © C Flanigan/Getty Images; page 49 (Taylor and her mum) ©
Cooper Neill/Getty Images for dcp; (Olivia Benson) © Raymond Hall/GC Images/Getty Images; page 50 (Taylor in *CSI*) © Eric Ford/
Shutterstock; page 50/51 (Bombalurina in *Cats*) © TCD/Prod.DB / Alamy Stock Photo; page 52 (*Reputation* album) © Patti McConville /
Alamy Stock Photo; page 53 (*Reputation* tour) © Kevin Mazur/TAS18/Getty Images for TAS; page 54 (Taylor talking about important
things) © CBS Photo Archive via Getty Images; page 55 (*Miss Americana*) © Netflix / Courtesy Everett Collection Inc / Alamy Stock Photo;
page 61 (Kanye West) © Christopher Polk/Getty Images

Printed in China

A CIP catalogue record for this book is available from the British Library

ISBN: 978-0-241-46326-0

All correspondence to:
Penguin Books
Penguin Random House Children's
One Embassy Gardens, 8 Viaduct Gardens,
London SW11 7BW

MIX
Paper | Supporting
responsible forestry
FSC® C018179
www.fsc.org

Contents

People in the book

Taylor Swift

Andrea Swift

Scott Swift

Austin Swift

Selena Gomez

Taylor's cat Olivia Benson (and her other cats, Meredith Grey and Benjamin Button)

New words

boyfriend

CD

fans

stadium

stage

Note about the book

Taylor Swift started singing at a very young age. She learned the guitar and started writing songs about her **life*** – her friends, her family and her **boyfriends**. Then she started singing for her friends and in **shows**. Today, Taylor is a very famous singer, with many **fans** in many countries. This is her story.

Before-reading questions

1 What do you know about Taylor Swift? Think about these questions:
   a Where was she born?
   b What is she famous for?
   c Which of her songs do you know? Do you like her songs?

2 Taylor Swift lived in Nashville. What do you know about Nashville? Think about these questions:
   a Where is Nashville?
   b What music is Nashville famous for?

3 Taylor Swift is famous. What is good about that? What is bad about that?

*Definitions of words in **bold** can be found in the glossary on pages 63–64

One night in Tokyo ...

It is evening in Tokyo, Japan, on the 21st November 2018.

More than 50,000 **fans** are at the Tokyo Dome **stadium**.

"TAYLOR! TAYLOR!" they sing.

Fans at the Tokyo Dome stadium

Then Taylor Swift comes on the **stage**.

The people in the stadium are very happy. Their favourite singer is here!

Taylor is finishing her *Reputation* **tour**.

Taylor on her *Reputation* tour

She sings her famous songs, and her fans know all the words.

Taylor smiles. She loves singing on the stage and meeting her many fans.

"Thank you, Tokyo!" she says.

Taylor Swift is a very famous singer in many countries. Let's learn more about her . . .

Taylor in Tokyo

CHAPTER ONE

Young Taylor

Taylor Alison Swift was **born** on the
13th December 1989.

Her parents are Andrea and Scott Swift.
They had important jobs in banks. The family
lived on a beautiful Christmas-tree **farm** in
Pennsylvania, in the United States of America.

A Christmas-tree farm

Taylor and Austin Swift

Taylor's brother, Austin, was born two years after Taylor.

Young Taylor and Austin were happy on the farm.

Taylor loved telling stories to her family about the animals on the farm.

Taylor's family had horses and a dog.

Taylor loved singing, too. She sang children's songs with her own words, and she could remember all the words to the songs in Disney films.

Taylor's family **moved** to the town of Wyomissing in Pennsylvania in 1998. She was nine years old.

Taylor moved to Wyomissing.

But Taylor did not like school in Wyomissing, because she did not have many friends.

One day, Taylor saw a **play** at the Berks Youth Theatre Academy. It was *Charlie and the Chocolate Factory* by Roald Dahl.

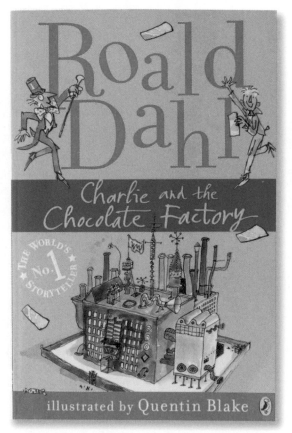

Charlie and the Chocolate Factory

Taylor loved the play, and she forgot about her **problems** at school.

A theatre

Taylor acted in plays with the Berks Youth
Theatre Academy.

Taylor sang it very well, and people loved it. Then she sang the national anthem at more sports games.

Taylor singing the US national anthem in 2002

Taylor sang in lots of places.

Now Taylor was a very good singer, and she wanted a **record deal**.

CHAPTER TWO

Nashville

One day, eleven-year-old Taylor watched a TV **show** about her favourite singer, Faith Hill. Faith Hill sings and **plays** country music – guitar music from the USA.

Faith Hill

Faith Hill and many country-music singers started in Nashville in the USA.

Nashville

Nashville is the home of country music. Lots of music **companies** have offices there.

Taylor liked singing songs by Dolly Parton, LeAnn Rimes and Shania Twain.

Dolly Parton

LeAnn Rimes

Shania Twain

Taylor sang her favourite songs and made a **CD**.

"Please can we take my CD to Nashville?"
Taylor asked her parents.

Taylor and her mum went to Music Row in Nashville. They went to lots of music companies and gave them Taylor's CD.

Music Square is in Music Row in Nashville.

But lots of singers go to Nashville with their CDs. They all want record deals.

Musicians in Nashville

Taylor and her mum went home and waited. But there were too many young singers, and too many CDs . . .

CHAPTER THREE

A different singer

Taylor with a guitar.

After Nashville, Taylor was sad. "How can I be different from the other singers?" she asked.

One day, she found an old guitar at home.

Taylor was now a singer and a guitar player.

Taylor began guitar lessons. She played the guitar every day, and she started writing songs.

Now Taylor could sing *and* play the guitar!

At fourteen years old, Taylor got her first **manager** – Dan Dymtrow. Dan saw Taylor play and liked her songs.

Dan Dymtrow

One day, Taylor went to Nashville with Dan, and she sang her songs for some music companies.

RCA, one of the big music companies, loved Taylor. They gave her an **Artist's Development Deal**.

RCA's office in Nashville

This deal helped Taylor with her singing and song writing.

Taylor's parents were happy about the Artist's Development Deal.

"Let's all move to Nashville," they said.

"Yes, please!" said Taylor.

Taylor's father moved his work to Nashville, and the family moved to Hendersonville, Tennessee, near Nashville.

Hendersonville, Tennessee

In Nashville, Taylor wrote new songs with a song **writer**, Liz Rose.

Taylor wrote beautiful songs about her **life** – her friends, **boyfriends**, family and school.

Liz Rose

Now Taylor had lots of country-music songs.

"Please can I make a CD, now?" Taylor asked RCA.

Taylor at fifteen

"No," they said. "You are too young, and you are not ready."

Taylor was very sad. "But I *am* ready!" she said. Taylor stopped her Artist's Development Deal with RCA.

The Bluebird Café

Then Taylor played at The Bluebird Café – a famous music place in Nashville.

A music manager, Scott Borchetta, saw Taylor there. He loved Taylor's singing and her songs.

Scott gave Taylor a record deal with his new music **company**, Big Machine Records.

Scott Borchetta

CHAPTER FOUR

Record deal

Taylor Swift was Big Machine Records'
first singer.

Taylor and Scott

Taylor was only fifteen, but she had
150 songs.

Tim McGraw

Taylor played her song "Tim McGraw" for
Scott. Tim McGraw is a famous country-music
singer – Taylor's song was about his music.

Scott loved it. "That's your first **single**!"
he said.

Taylor wrote songs about her life because it helped her with her problems.

Young people loved her music because it helped them, too.

Young Taylor singing her songs

Taylor's Instagram page

Taylor made social-media pages for her music and talked to young people on social media.

Taylor's fans loved her pages, and she quickly got more young fans.

In October 2006, sixteen-year-old Taylor made her first **album** – *Taylor Swift*.

She wrote all eleven songs on it.

Taylor went on television a lot. She sang songs and talked about her album. She was great!

Taylor on television

Many people heard Taylor's album and loved it.

Two of Taylor's favourite country-music singers heard it, too – Faith Hill and Tim McGraw. Now they were Taylor Swift fans!

Taylor with Faith Hill and Tim McGraw

Taylor on Faith and Tim's tour

In 2007, Taylor sang on Faith and Tim's tour.

Taylor's third single, "Our Song", was one of the top country-music songs in the USA.

In 2007, seventeen-year-old
Taylor got a country-music
award for her "Tim McGraw"
music **video**.

Taylor with her award

40

Taylor went to the Grammys in 2008, too – the Grammys is a big music awards show in the USA.

She did not get a Grammy award. But she walked on the red carpet and met lots of famous people!

Taylor at the Grammys in 2008

CHAPTER FIVE

Taylor is famous

In 2009, nineteen-year-old Taylor went on her first big tour. It was for her second album, *Fearless*.

Taylor on her *Fearless* tour

She travelled to stadiums in the USA, and to Canada, England, Australia and Japan, too.

Taylor singing in a stadium

Taylor sang night after night.

Taylor's fans loved her *Fearless* tour, and they wanted more big tours!

Taylor loved her fans – her "Swifties" – and they loved her.

Taylor and her Swifties

Some nights, Taylor had a "T-Party" ("Taylor-Party") for some of her fans on her tour.

Fans at the T-Party had food and drinks with Taylor after she sang.

Taylor and her fans at a T-Party

In 2009, Taylor got an MTV Video Music Award. She went on the stage.

"Thank you . . ." she said – but she did not finish her sentence.

The singer Kanye West came on the stage, too. "But Beyoncé's video was great!" he said.

Kanye West on the stage

Taylor was very sad! Beyoncé was angry.

Beyoncé and Taylor

Beyoncé got a different award that night and said, "Come on the stage with me, Taylor."

Taylor got on the stage, and she thanked people for her award.

Selena and Taylor

Kanye did not like Taylor, but lots of people did. Taylor's friends are very important to her.

One of Taylor's good friends is Selena Gomez. She is a singer, too.

Taylor, Selena and their friends have great parties together!

Taylor's friends

Taylor's mum is always there for her, too.

Taylor and her mum

Taylor has three more good friends – her cats, Mcredith Grey, Olivia Benson and Benjamin Button.

**Taylor with her cat
Olivia Benson**

Taylor in *CSI*

Taylor is not only a singer – she is a good **actor**, too.

In 2009, she was in *CSI*, one of her favourite TV shows.

Next, she was in movies – she was in *Hannah Montana* (2009), *Valentine's Day* (2010) and *Cats* (2019).

Taylor was Bombalurina in *Cats*.

Taylor's first three albums were country music, but her next four – *Red*, *1989*, *Reputation* and *Lover* – were **pop** albums.

Taylor's *Reputation* album

Taylor's first pop single was "We Are Never Ever Getting Back Together". She wrote it about an old boyfriend.

Taylor's fans loved her new music, and many new fans loved it, too.

Taylor was now a famous pop singer.

Taylor on her *Reputation* tour

People know many things about Taylor Swift – she is a singer, writer and actor. But Taylor does other wonderful things, too . . .

Taylor talking about important things in her life

She gives money to **charities** and speaks about important things.

In 2020, Taylor made a movie about her life and **politics** – *Miss Americana.*

Taylor in her movie, *Miss Americana*

After many years as a famous singer, Taylor learned a lot about life. She worked hard, and now she has many fans, great songs and big awards. She has wonderful friends and family, too.

What is next for Taylor Swift? She is still very young, and this is only the first part of her story!

During-reading questions

Write the answers to these questions in your notebook.

CHAPTER ONE

1 What did Taylor do in Tokyo?
2 Who is in Taylor's family?
3 Where did Taylor's family live?
4 Where did the family move?
5 Taylor saw a play at the Berks Youth Theatre Academy. What was it?
6 What song did Taylor sing at a sports game?

CHAPTER TWO

1 Where did Faith Hill start singing?
2 Whose songs did Taylor like singing?
3 Where did Taylor take her CD? Why did she take it there?
4 What did Taylor do after Nashville?

CHAPTER THREE

1 How was Taylor different from other singers?
2 Who is Dan Dymtrow?
3 Who gave Taylor an Artist's Development Deal? What was it?
4 What did Liz Rose and Taylor do together?
5 Where did Taylor meet Scott Borchetta?
6 What did Big Machine Records give Taylor?

CHAPTER FOUR

1 Taylor's first single was "Tim McGraw". Who is Tim McGraw?
2 What did Taylor do on television?
3 Taylor got her first country-music award in 2007. How old was she, and what was the award for?
4 What is the "Grammys"?

CHAPTER FIVE

1 Which album was Taylor's first big tour for?
2 What are "Swifties", and what is a "T-Party"?
3 Beyoncé said, "Come on the stage with me, Taylor." What happened next?
4 Who is Selena Gomez?
5 "Taylor's mum is always there for her, too." What does this mean, do you think?
6 What was Taylor's first pop single? What is it about?

After-reading questions

1 Who are these people?
   a Scott Swift
   b Scott Borchetta
   c Meredith Grey
   d Bombalurina

2 What does Taylor write her songs about? Why does she do this, do you think?

3 Think of some famous singers and song writers. What do you like or not like about their music? Are they different? Why?

4 What is Taylor's movie, *Miss Americana*, about?

5 What new things did you learn about Taylor Swift in this book?

Exercises

CHAPTER ONE

1 Are these sentences *true* or *false*? Write the correct answers in your notebook.

1 Taylor's family lived on a pig farm. ....*false*...........
2 Austin is Taylor's brother.
3 Taylor had horses.
4 Taylor could not remember the words to the songs in Disney films.
5 Taylor sang a Dolly Parton song at a sports game.

2 Write the correct question word. Then answer the questions in your notebook.

1 ....*Where*......... did Taylor's family live?
   On a Christmas-tree farm...........
2 .... is Taylor's mum?
3 .... play did Taylor see at the Berks Youth Theatre Academy?
4 .... did Taylor forget about her problems at school?
5 .... did Taylor want?

CHAPTER TWO

3 Put these sentences in the correct order in your notebook.

a .... Taylor and her mum went to Nashville.
b .... Taylor sang her favourite songs and made a CD.
c ...*1*.... Taylor watched a TV show about Faith Hill.
d .... Taylor went home and waited.
e .... Taylor gave her CD to music companies in Nashville.

CHAPTER THREE

4 Complete these sentences in your notebook, using the words from the box.

guitar	companies	life
writer	manager	

1 Taylor played the ....*guitar*......... every day.
2 Dan Dymtrow was Taylor's first ....
3 Taylor sang her songs for some music .... in Nashville.
4 Liz Rose is a song ....
5 Taylor wrote beautiful songs about her ....

5 Order the words to make sentences in your notebook.

1 guitar / began / lessons / Taylor /
Taylor began guitar lessons.
2 Nashville / to / Taylor / went /
3 family / The / to / moved / Hendersonville /
4 songs / Taylor / with / wrote / Liz / Rose /
5 sad / was / very / Taylor /

CHAPTER FOUR

6 Write the past simple tense of these verbs in your notebook.

1 Taylor ...*was*... (be) Big Machine Records' first singer.
2 Taylor .... (play) her song "Tim McGraw" for Scott Borchetta.
3 Taylor's fans .... (love) her social-media page.
4 Taylor .... (sing) on Faith Hill and Tim McGraw's tour.
5 Taylor .... (get) a country-music award.
6 Taylor .... (go) to the Grammys in 2008.

CHAPTER FIVE

7 Look at the picture, and answer these questions in your notebook.

1 Who is talking to Taylor?
   Kanye West

2 What is he doing?

3 What is he saying?

4 What is Taylor thinking? Is she happy or sad?

8 Write the opposites of these words in your notebook.

1 night ....*day*............   2 big

3 sad   4 different

5 good   6 always

61

Project work

1 You are Taylor Swift. Write a diary page about a day in your life on tour.

2 Watch Taylor's movie, *Miss Americana*. Write a film review about it. Did you like it? Why/Why not?

3 Write some words for a country-music or pop song about your life.

4 Write a paragraph about Taylor Swift in your own words. For example, *Taylor Swift was born in . . .*

5 You are meeting Taylor Swift. Think of questions for her. Write them in your notebook.

Glossary

actor (n.)
a person in a film, *play* or
television *show*

album (n.)
An *album* has songs on it. You
buy a singer's *album*.

Artist's Development Deal
(pr. n.)
A *company* gives an *Artist's
Development Deal* to a person.
It helps the person with
their music.

born (adj.)
A baby comes out from its
mother's body. It is *born*.

boyfriend (n.)
Your *boyfriend* is a man or boy.
You love him or like him a lot.

CD (n.)
A *CD* has songs on it. You buy
it in a flat box.

charity (n.)
A *charity* helps poor people or
ill people. People give money
to *charities*.

company (n.)
A *company* makes and sells
things. People work for a
company. We say "*companies*"
for two or more of them.

fans (n.)
Fans like a famous person
very much.

farm (n.)
A person grows plants on a *farm*
or has animals on a *farm*.

life (n.)
from the start of living, to the
end of living. This is your *life*.

manager (n.)
A singer or an *actor* has a
manager. The *manager* finds work
for them and helps them with
money.

move (v.)
to go to a different place and
live there

national anthem (n.)
the song of a country

play (n. and v.)
Actors act a story. This is a *play*.
You often see a *play* at a theatre.
A person can also *play* music.
They *play* a guitar, etc.

politics (pl. n.)
the work of the government
(= important people. They say
what must happen in a country.)

pop (adj.)
fast music. Young people often like *pop* music because they can dance to it.

problems (n.)
You have *problems*. They make you sad.

record deal (n.)
A *company* gives a *record deal* to a singer. Then the *company* sells the singer's music.

show (n.)
You watch a *show* on television or in a theatre.

single (n.)
A *single* is one song. An *album* is many songs. People can buy a singer's *single* or *album*.

stadium (n.)
a large place with many seats for football or music *shows*

stage (n.)
People sing or act *plays* on a *stage*.

tour (n.)
A singer goes to many places. They sing in front of many people. They do a *tour*.

video (n.)
a film. A singer sings their song in it.

writer (n.)
A song *writer* writes songs.